Jawed Karim

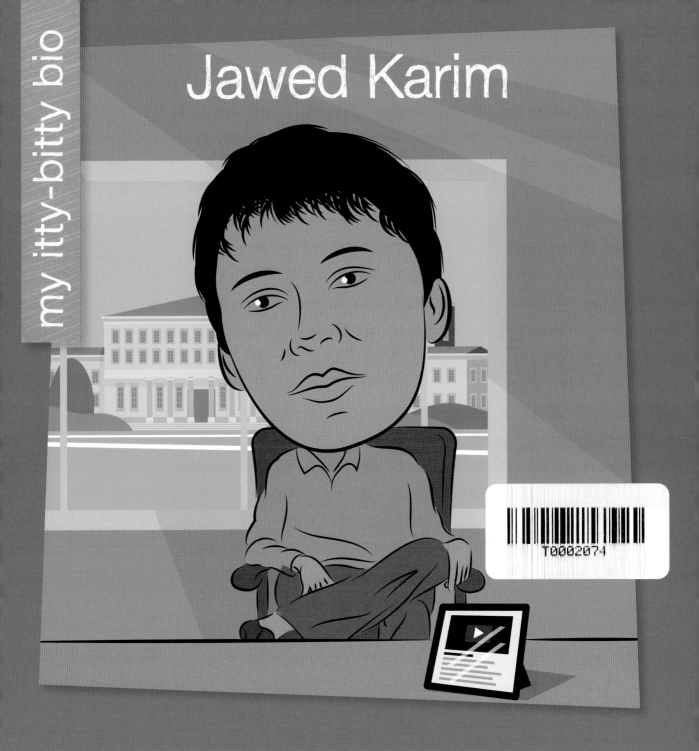

T0002074

CHERRY LAKE PRESS

Published in the United States of America by Cherry Lake Publishing Group
Ann Arbor, Michigan
www.cherrylakepublishing.com

Reading Adviser: Beth Walker Gambro, MS, Ed., Reading Consultant, Yorkville, IL
Book Designer: Jennifer Wahi
Illustrator: Jeff Bane

Photo Credits: page 5: © ArTono/Shutterstock; page 7: © New Africa/Shutterstock; pages 9, 22: © Saibal Ghosh/Shutterstock; page 11: © REDPIXEL.PL/Shutterstock; pages 13, 23: © tomeqs/Shutterstock; page 15: © Martin Klimek/ZUMA Press/Alamy Stock Photo; page 17: © Pato Lucas/Shutterstock; page 19: Jawed Karim/YouTube; page 21: Robin Brown/Wikimedia Commons

Cherry Lake Press is an imprint of Cherry Lake Publishing Group.

Library of Congress Cataloging-in-Publication Data

Names: Loh-Hagan, Virginia, author. | Bane, Jeff, illustrator.
Title: Jawed Karim / by Virginia Loh-Hagan ; illustrated by Jeff Bane.
Description: Ann Arbor : Cherry Lake Publishing, 2023. | Series: My
   itty-bitty bio | Audience: Grades K-1 | Summary: "This biography for
   early readers examines the life of Muslim Jawed Karim, co-founder of
   YouTube, in a simple, age-appropriate way that helps young readers
   develop word recognition and reading skills. Includes table of contents,
   author biography, timeline, glossary, index, and other informative
   backmatter. The My Itty-Bitty Bio series celebrates diversity, covering
   women and men from a range of backgrounds and professions including
   immigrants and individuals with disabilities"-- Provided by publisher.
Identifiers: LCCN 2022042680 | ISBN 9781668919194 (hardcover) | ISBN
   9781668920213 (paperback) | ISBN 9781668921548 (ebook) | ISBN
   9781668922873 (pdf)
Subjects: LCSH: Karim, Jawed, 1979---Juvenile literature. | YouTube
   (Firm)--Juvenile literature. | YouTube (Electronic resource)--Juvenile
   literature. | Telecommunications engineers--United
   States--Biography--Juvenile literature. | Webmasters--United
   States--Biography--Juvenile literature. | Computer programmers--United
   States--Biography--Juvenile literature. | Internet videos--Juvenile
   literature. | Online social networks--Juvenile literature.
Classification: LCC TK5102.56.K36 L64 2023 | DDC 338.7/610053092
   [B]--dc23/eng/20221017
LC record available at https://lccn.loc.gov/2022042680

Printed in the United States of America
Corporate Graphics

table of contents

About the author: When not writing, Dr. Virginia Loh-Hagan serves as the Director of the Asian Pacific Islander Desi American (APIDA) Center at San Diego State University. She identifies as Chinese American and is committed to amplifying APIDA communities. She lives in San Diego with her very tall husband and very naughty dogs.

About the illustrator: Jeff Bane and his two business partners own a studio along the American River in Folsom, California, home of the 1849 Gold Rush. When Jeff's not sketching or illustrating for clients, he's either swimming or kayaking in the river to relax.

I was born in 1979 in Germany. My mother is German. My father is South Asian. I have a younger **sibling**.

We moved around a lot when I was younger. People didn't like our family. We looked different.

We finally moved to the United States. We moved to Minnesota. I did well in school. I liked learning. I liked solving problems. I wanted to learn more about computers.

What do you like to study?

I worked in **technology**. I learned a lot. I solved problems.

Sharing computer videos was hard. There were many steps. I wanted an easier way.

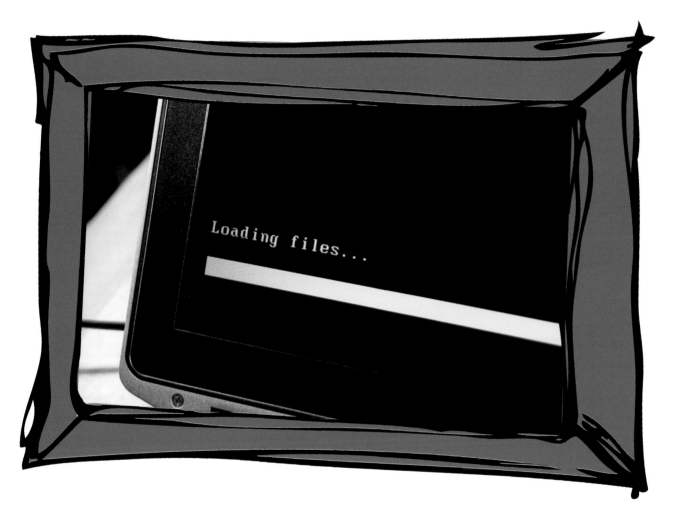

I helped create **YouTube**.
I made the first **home page**.
I **posted** the first video.

What are your favorite
videos to watch online?

The video was of me. I was at a zoo. There were two elephants. I talked about their trunks.

My video was short. It was from real life. People liked it.

I changed how people view videos. Anyone can make videos. Any moment can be special.

What would you like to ask me?

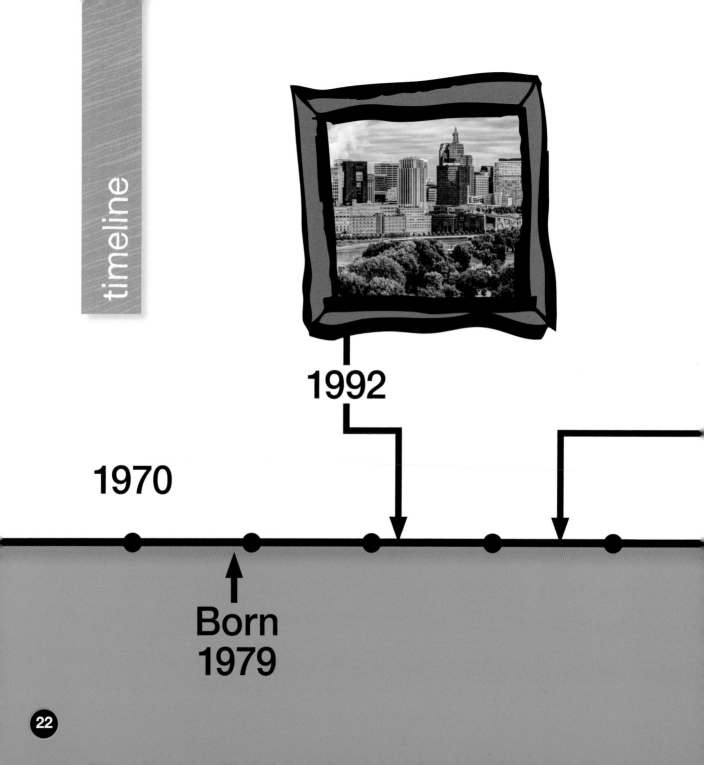

1992

1970

Born
1979

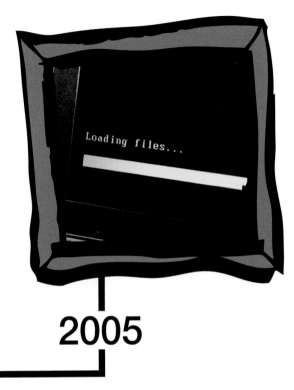

Loading files...

2005

2070

glossary

home page (HOHM PAYJ) a personal account on YouTube; also called a channel

posted (POH-stuhd) added online

sibling (SIH-bling) brother or sister

technology (tek-NAH-luh-jee) the use of computers

YouTube (YOO-toob) an online video sharing platform

index